OECD Best Practice Principles for Regulatory Policy

Regulatory Impact Assessment

This document, as well as any data and map included herein, are without prejudice to the status of or sovereignty over any territory, to the delimitation of international frontiers and boundaries and to the name of any territory, city or area.

Please cite this publication as:
OECD (2020), *Regulatory Impact Assessment*, OECD Best Practice Principles for Regulatory Policy, OECD Publishing, Paris, *https://doi.org/10.1787/7a9638cb-en*.

ISBN 978-92-64-42294-0 (print)
ISBN 978-92-64-80111-0 (pdf)

OECD Best Practice Principles for Regulatory Policy
ISSN 2311-6005 (print)
ISSN 2311-6013 (online)

Photo credits: Cover © Julia Sudnitskaya/Shutterstock.com

Corrigenda to publications may be found on line at: *www.oecd.org/about/publishing/corrigenda.htm*.
© OECD 2020

The use of this work, whether digital or print, is governed by the Terms and Conditions to be found at *http://www.oecd.org/termsandconditions*.

Foreword

This report is part of a series of "best practice principles" produced under the auspices of the OECD Regulatory Policy Committee.

Regulations are indispensable for the proper functioning of economies and societies. They create the "rules of the game" for citizens, business, government and civil society. They underpin markets, protect the rights and safety of citizens and ensure the delivery of public goods and services. The objective of regulatory policy is to ensure that the regulatory "lever" works effectively, so that regulations and regulatory frameworks work in the public interest.

The quality of the regulatory environment and the delivery of regulatory outcomes is strongly dependent on the quality of processes for designing regulations. If used systematically and across the whole of government, regulatory impact assessment (RIA) can ensure better-quality government intervention. In addition, documenting and publishing the evidence and analysis used to design interventions can enhance accountability and transparency in the policy-making and decision-making processes.

The OECD has played a leading international role in promoting regulatory reform and sound regulatory practices across the whole of government. The 2012 *OECD Recommendation of the Council on Regulatory Policy and Governance* summarises the information and experience it has gathered.

Building on this wealth of information and practices, these Principles provide a synthetic tool to help decision makers, policy makers, civil servants and other practitioners in the public sector internationally better design and implement their RIA systems and strategies.

This document was approved by the Regulatory Policy Committee at its 21st Session on 6 November 2019 and prepared for publication by the OECD Secretariat.

Acknowledgements

These principles were prepared by the OECD Public Governance Directorate (GOV), under the leadership of Marcos Bonturi, Director. They were drafted by Daniel Trnka, OECD Senior Policy Analyst, under the supervision of Nick Malyshev, Head of the Regulatory Policy Division, GOV. Jennifer Stein co-ordinated the editorial process.

Thanks are extended to all members of the Regulatory Policy Committee who provided substantial comments and support to the various drafts of the principles paper. Extensive and useful comments were provided in the public consultation by Mr. Jonathan Ayto, New Zealand Treasury; Mr. Paolo Paruolo, Joint Research Centre, European Commission; Ms Fabiola Perales, expert on regulatory policy, Mexico and Mr. Yoav Teitelbaum, National Cyber Directorate, Israel.

Table of contents

Executive summary	6
1 Background and context	**8**
Rationale and goal of the principles	8
Notes	12
References	13
2 Best practice principles for regulatory impact analysis	**14**
Commitment and buy-in for RIA	16
Governance of RIA – having the right set up or system design	18
Embedding RIA through strengthening capacity and accountability of the administration	20
Targeted and appropriate RIA methodology	21
Continuous monitoring, evaluation and improvement of RIA	29
Notes	32
References	33

Executive summary

Regulation is an important tool for achieving governments' social, economic and environmental policy objectives. Governments have a broad range of regulatory instruments reflecting the complex and diverse needs of their citizens, communities and economy.

The quality of both the regulatory environment and regulatory outcomes is strongly dependent on the quality of processes for designing regulations. When developing interventions, whether policies, laws, regulations or other types of "rule", governments do not always fully consider their likely effects. In addition, government intervention has costs, which might, in some cases, outweigh the anticipated benefits. As a result, there are many instances of unintended consequences and, ultimately, negative impacts for citizens, businesses and society as a whole that essentially result from badly designed interventions. Often, these negative impacts are felt more by smaller, unorganised, hard-to-reach, less informed or marginalised constituents in society. They are thus detrimental to achieving inclusive growth, sustainable development, building trust and maintaining the integrity of the rule of law.

Regulatory impact assessment provides decision makers with crucial information on whether and how to regulate to achieve public policy goals. RIA also helps policy makers defend decisions not to intervene in markets where the costs of doing so outweigh the benefits. RIA further helps defend policy makers' decisions by demonstrating that there are benefits to regulation – something that is often overlooked by society and governments.

The Principles provide policy makers, civil servants and other public sector practitioners with a practical instrument for better designing and implementing RIA systems and strategies. The Principles cover a wide range of institutional organisations, tools and practices and present a list of critical steps, as well as "dos and don'ts" for developing RIA frameworks.

As a minimum, every process of regulatory impact assessment should include these elements: problem definition, objective, description of the regulatory proposal, identification of alternatives, analysis of benefit and costs, identification of the preferred solution and setting out the monitoring and evaluation framework.

For RIA to be successful, it needs to:

- Always start at the inception phase of the regulation-making process;
- Clearly identify the problem and desired goals of the proposal;
- Identify and evaluate all potential alternative solutions (including non-regulatory ones);
- Always attempt to assess all potential costs and benefits, both direct and indirect;
- Be based on all available evidence and scientific expertise;
- Be developed transparently with stakeholders, and have the results clearly communicated.

The Principles are organised under the following five topics:

- Commitment and buy-in for RIA – creating credible "internal and external constraints" that guarantee that RIA will effectively be implemented, securing political and stakeholders' support and ensuring transparency of decision making to enable public control of the RIA process;

- Governance of RIA/having the right set-up or system design – including integration with other regulatory management tools, adjusting to the legal and administrative system and culture of the country, ensuring quality oversight and an approach proportional to the significance of the regulation, and allocating responsibilities for IRA;
- Embedding RIA by strengthening the capacity and accountability of the administration – providing guidance and training and limiting exceptions;
- Targeted and appropriate RIA methodology – providing simple and flexible methodology, defining the policy context and objectives, taking into account all plausible alternatives, identifying all relevant direct and important indirect costs as well as benefits, developing strategies on collecting and accessing data, communicating results of RIA, and engaging with stakeholders throughout the RIA process;
- Continuous evaluation and improvement of RIA - validating the real impacts of adopted regulations after their implementation and comprehensive evaluation of the RIA framework and oversight bodies.

The Principles complement the 2012 *Recommendation of the Council on Regulatory Policy and Governance*. They can be used by OECD member and non-member countries to guide their reforms. They will be also used by the OECD Secretariat when reviewing regulatory policies in member and non-member countries.

1 Background and context

This paper is part of a series of reports on 'best practice principles' produced under the auspices of the OECD Regulatory Policy Committee. As with other reports in the series, it provides an extension and elaboration of principles highlighted in the *2012 Recommendation of the Council on Regulatory Policy and Governance* (OECD, 2012[1]).

The principles are intended to be relevant and useful to all member governments. They thus offer general guidance rather than providing detailed prescription. Nevertheless, in seeking to invoke "best practice" the principles are intentionally ambitious. Few if any countries could be expected at this point to meet them all. However, they are also grounded in the actual experience of different countries, so should not be seen as unattainable or merely aspirational. At the same time, the OECD understands that there are limits to the absorptive capacity of policy makers to implement all requirements for RIA implementation. Governments should use an approach that will not just widen the gap between what exists "on paper" and the actual implementation. It is important to make sure that policies are implemented in practices rather to update them to "tick all the boxes" in the Principles.

In some elements, the principles might slightly overlap with other best practice principles published by the Regulatory Policy Committee, especially the principles on stakeholder engagement and on *ex post* reviews of regulation. These sets of principles should be logically interconnected and implementing each other with references to other sets where needed.

Rationale and goal of the principles

Evidence-based policy making is a well understood and accepted tenet of good governance. Policies and/or regulations should be always based on the best available information, data, analysis and scientific expertise and take into account all potential alternative solutions to a problem. However, government interventions, whether they are a policy, law, regulation or other type of "rule", do not always fully consider their likely effects at the time of their development. In addition, government intervention has costs and there might be cases where those costs might outweigh the anticipated benefits. As a result, there are many instances of unintended consequences and ultimately negative impacts for citizens, businesses and society as a whole that could be avoided, and essentially result from badly designed interventions. Often, these negative impacts are felt more by smaller, unorganised, hard-to-reach, less well informed or marginalised constituents in society, which is detrimental to achieving inclusive growth, sustainable development, building trust and maintaining the integrity of the rule of law.

The policy-making environment has also become more complex and fast paced. Digital and shared economies, innovative industries, technological advancements, social media and not to mention the move of governments towards digitalisation have created challenges for ensuring and maintaining quality or at least fit-for-purpose regulatory frameworks. This is often within the context of limited public sector resources and increasing demands on administration.

If used systematically and as a government-wide approach, regulatory impact assessment (RIA) provides a critical tool to ensure greater quality of government intervention. In addition, the documentation and publication of the evidence and analysis to design interventions provides the opportunity to enhance accountability and transparency in the policy-making and decision-making processes. Regulatory impact assessment provides crucial information to decision makers on whether and how to regulate to achieve public policy goals (OECD, 2012[1]). It is challenging to develop "correct" policy responses which also maximise societal well-being. It is the role of RIA to help assist with this, by critically examining the impacts and consequences of a range of alternative options. Improving the evidence base for regulation through RIA is one of the most important regulatory tools available to governments (OECD, 2012[1]).[1]

RIA also helps policymakers to defend decisions not to intervene in markets where the costs of doing so outweigh the benefits. RIA further helps defend policymakers' decisions by presenting that there are in fact benefits to regulation – something that is often overlooked by society and governments. Implementing a functioning RIA framework might therefore represent an important step in a policy-change from 'deregulation' to more systemic 'better' or 'smart regulation'.

The motivations for implementing RIA in some countries might also, either explicitly or implicitly, include a desire to impose greater discipline on the quasi-independent regulators and agencies with delegated powers to regulate, to increase democratic accountability of administrations, or even the bias against regulation (or, more narrowly, a desire to minimise compliance costs for business) or just international pressure. This document will mostly focus on the evidence-based policy-making rationale.

The use of RIA can also be viewed by government officials as a key part of the exercise of their professional responsibility to try to reduce the impact of their inevitable behavioural biases and errors on their analysis and advice, which might include:

- framing and anchoring effects (our conclusions are affected by how the problem is framed, or our recent experience);
- conformance and group-think (we trust those we like, and we generally wish to avoid conflict or maintain group solidarity);
- over-confidence and optimism bias (we fail to identify knowledge gaps, and fail to assess what could go wrong);
- confirmation bias and motivated reasoning (we amplify what suits us, and ignore or reinterpret what does not).

The evidence shows many challenges and shortcomings of RIA implementation. As pointed out in the 2018 Regulatory Policy Outlook, in many instances "RIA has become over-procedural and is not targeted to the most significant laws and regulations, either because there is no triage system or because regulatory proposals with significant impacts are exempted. Where assessments are undertaken, they often focus on narrowly defined economic impacts, such as regulatory burdens for business, ignoring other significant effects" (OECD, 2018[2]).

The OECD has produced a wide range of documents on RIA (see Box 1). In addition, the OECD Regulatory Reform Reviews of countries along with country programmes supporting RIA implementation have provided in-depth understanding of RIA "in the field". The 2015 and 2018 Regulatory Policy Outlooks have provided further data on how RIA is being implemented and the challenges as well as successful strategies that are being utilised. Also, there is new evidence collected from the application of RIA to specific areas such as inclusive growth, trade, environmental policy and transport (Deighton-Smith, Erbacci and Kauffmann, 2016[3]); (Basedow and Kauffmann, 2016[4]).

> **Box 1. OECD publications on regulatory impact assessment**
>
> (OECD, 2018[2]), OECD Regulatory Policy Outlook 2018, Paris, https://doi.org/10.1787/9789264303072-en.
>
> (OECD, 2017[5]), "Chile Evaluation Report: Regulatory Impact Assessment", OECD Reviews of Regulatory Reform, Paris, http://www.oecd.org/gov/regulatory-policy/Chile-Evaluation-Full-Report-web.pdf.
>
> (Deighton-Smith, Erbacci and Kauffmann, 2016[3]), "Promoting inclusive growth through better regulation: The role of regulatory impact assessment", OECD Regulatory Policy Working Papers, No. 3, Paris, https://doi.org/10.1787/5jm3tqwqp1vj-en.
>
> (OECD, 2015[6]), OECD Regulatory Policy Outlook 2015, Paris, https://doi.org/10.1787/9789264238770-en.
>
> (OECD, 2015[7]), Regulatory Policy in Perspective: A Reader's Companion to the OECD Regulatory Policy Outlook 2015, Paris, https://doi.org/10.1787/9789264241800-en.
>
> (Jacob, Ferretti and Guske, 2012[8]), Sustainability in Impact Assessments: A Review of Impact Assessment Systems in Selected OECD Countries and the European Commission, OECD Publishing, Paris, http://www.oecd.org/gov/regulatory-policy/sustainability%20in%20impact%20assessment%20sg-sd(2011)6-final.pdf.
>
> (OECD, 2012[1]), Recommendation of the Council on Regulatory Policy and Governance, OECD Publishing, Paris, http://dx.doi.org/10.1787/9789264209022-en.
>
> (Klaus et al., 2011[9]), Integrating the Environment in Regulatory Impact Assessments, Paris, http://www.oecd.org/gov/regulatory-policy/Integrating%20RIA%20in%20Decision%20Making.pdf.
>
> (OECD, 2009[10]), Regulatory Impact Analysis: A Tool for Policy Coherence, Paris, http://dx.doi.org/10.1787/9789264067110-en.
>
> (OECD, 2008[11]), Introductory Handbook for Undertaking Regulatory Impact Analysis (RIA), OECD Publishing, Paris, http://www.oecd.org/gov/regulatory-policy/44789472.pdf.
>
> (OECD, 2008[12]), Building an Institutional Framework for Regulatory Impact Analysis (RIA): Guidance for Policy Makers, Paris, http://www.oecd.org/regreform/regulatory-policy/40984990.pdf.
>
> (Rodrigo, 2005[13]), Regulatory Impact Analysis in OECD Countries Challenges for developing countries, Paris, http://www.oecd.org/gov/regulatory-policy/35258511.pdf.
>
> (OECD, 2004[14]), Regulatory Impact Analysis (RIA) Inventory, Paris, http://www.oecd.org/gov/regulatory-policy/35258430.pdf.
>
> (OECD, 1997[15]), Regulatory Impact Analysis: Best Practices in OECD Countries, Paris, https://doi.org/10.1787/9789264162150-en.

The Principles aim to gather and build on this wealth of relevant information and practices in a synthetic tool to provide decision-makers, policy-makers, civil servants and other practitioners in the public sector internationally with a practical instrument to better design and implement their RIA systems and strategies. While the Principles cover the wide range of institutional organisation, tools and practices that support a working RIA system, it is clear that countries may face more challenges in the implementation of some areas than in the others. There may also be value in presenting countries with a critical list of the critical steps and the Dos and Don'ts in relation to the development of their RIA framework. Keeping this in mind, it is proposed that the principles be accompanied by annexes focusing on specific aspects of the development of a RIA system that are proving more challenging for countries, for example, how to develop a proportionate approach to RIAs, how to assess the significance of impacts, what key elements should be in place to initiate a RIA framework. These annexes will be developed at a later stage after discussion with delegates on their relevance.

The objective of the Principles is not to replace the *2012 Recommendation on Regulatory and Policy Governance* (especially Principle No. 4 - see Box 2) but to rather complement and support the implementation of the Recommendation by providing more practically oriented and more specific guidance using the experience and information gathered through the work on both Regulatory Policy Outlooks an the country reviews.

> **Box 2. The 2012 OECD Recommendation on Regulatory and Policy Governance: Principle 4**
>
> *Integrate Regulatory Impact Assessment (RIA) into the early stages of the policy process for the formulation of new regulatory proposals. Clearly identify policy goals, and evaluate if regulation is necessary and how it can be most effective and efficient in achieving those goals. Consider means other than regulation and identify the tradeoffs of the different approaches analysed to identify the best approach.*
>
> 4.1. Adopt *ex ante* impact assessment practices that are proportional to the significance of the regulation, and include benefit cost analyses that consider the welfare impacts of regulation taking into account economic, social and environmental impacts including the distributional effects over time, identifying who is likely to benefit and who is likely to bear costs.
>
> 4.2. *Ex ante* assessment policies should require the identification of a specific policy need, and the objective of the regulation such as the correction of a market failure, or the need to protect citizen's rights that justifies the use of regulation.
>
> 4.3. *Ex ante* assessment policies should include a consideration of alternative ways of addressing the public policy objectives, including regulatory and non-regulatory alternatives to identify and select the most appropriate instrument, or mix of instruments to achieve policy goals. The no action option or baseline scenario should always be considered. *Ex ante* assessment should in most cases identify approaches likely to deliver the greatest net benefit to society, including complementary approaches such as through a combination of regulation, education and voluntary standards.
>
> 4.4. When regulatory proposals would have significant impacts, *ex ante* assessment of costs, benefits and risks should be quantitative whenever possible. Regulatory costs include direct costs (administrative, financial and capital costs) as well as indirect costs (opportunity costs) whether borne by businesses, citizens or government. *Ex ante* assessments should, where relevant, provide qualitative descriptions of those impacts that are difficult or impossible to quantify, such as equity, fairness, and distributional effects.
>
> 4.4. Regulatory impact analysis should as far as possible be made publicly available along with regulatory proposals. The analysis should be prepared in a suitable form and within adequate time to gain input from stakeholders and assist political decision-making. Good practice would involve using the Regulatory Impact Analysis as part of the consultation process.

> 4.5. *Ex ante* assessment policies should indicate that regulation should seek to enhance, not deter, competition and consumer welfare, and that to the extent that regulations dictated by public interest benefits may affect the competitive process, authorities should explore ways to limit adverse effects and carefully evaluate them against the claimed benefits of the regulation. This includes exploring whether the objectives of the regulation cannot be achieved by other less restrictive means.
>
> 4.6. When carrying out an assessment, officials should:
>
> - Assess economic, social and environmental impacts (where possible in quantitative and monetised terms), taking into account possible long term and spatial effects;
> - Evaluate if the adoption of common international instruments will efficiently address the identified policy issues and foster coherence at a global level with minimal disruption to national and international markets;
> - Evaluate the impact on small to medium sized enterprises and demonstrate how administrative and compliance costs are minimised.
>
> 4.7. RIA should be supported with clear policies, training programmes, guidance and quality control mechanisms for data collection and use. It should be integrated early in the processes for the development of policy and supported within agencies and at the centre of government.
>
> Source: (OECD, 2012[1]), Recommendation of the Council on Regulatory Policy and Governance, Paris, https://doi.org/10.1787/9789264209022-en.

Annexes to these Principles will be developed and published on the OECD website[2] covering the following issues:

- Setting thresholds and proportionality of RIA
- The oversight on the quality of RIA
- Quantifying benefits
- RIA and innovation – innovation tests
- Behavioural insights and RIA
- RIA and international regulatory co-operation

Notes

[1] RIA could usefully cover more than just regulations. Strategic policy choices, spending programmes, negotiation mandates, and other types of policy decisions may also benefit from RIA. This, however, goes beyond the scope of these Principles.

[2] http://oe.cd/regpol.

References

Basedow, R. and C. Kauffmann (2016), "International Trade and Good Regulatory Practices: Assessing The Trade Impacts of Regulation", *OECD Regulatory Policy Working Papers*, No. 4, OECD Publishing, Paris, http://dx.doi.org/10.1787/5jlv59hdgtf5-en. [4]

Deighton-Smith, R., A. Erbacci and C. Kauffmann (2016), "Promoting inclusive growth through better regulation: The role of regulatory impact assessment", *OECD Regulatory Policy Working Papers*, No. 3, OECD Publishing, Paris, https://dx.doi.org/10.1787/5jm3tqwqp1vj-en. [3]

Jacob, K., J. Ferretti and A. Guske (2012), *Sustainability in Impact Assessments: A Review of Impact Assessment Systems in selected OECD countries and the European Commission*, OECD, http://www.oecd.org/gov/regulatory-policy/Sustainability%20in%20impact%20assessment%20SG-SD(2011)6-final.pdf. [8]

Klaus, J. et al. (2011), *Integrating the Environment in Regulatory Impact Assessments*, OECD, http://www.oecd.org/gov/regulatory-policy/Integrating%20RIA%20in%20Decision%20Making.pdf. [9]

OECD (2018), *OECD Regulatory Policy Outlook 2018*, OECD Publishing, Paris, https://dx.doi.org/10.1787/9789264303072-en. [2]

OECD (2017), *Chile Evaluation Report: Regulatory Impact Assessment*, http://www.oecd.org/gov/regulatory-policy/Chile-Evaluation-Full-Report-web.pdf. [5]

OECD (2015), *OECD Regulatory Policy Outlook 2015*, OECD Publishing, Paris, https://dx.doi.org/10.1787/9789264238770-en. [6]

OECD (2015), *Regulatory Policy in Perspective: A Reader's Companion to the OECD Regulatory Policy Outlook 2015*, OECD Publishing, Paris, https://dx.doi.org/10.1787/9789264241800-en. [7]

OECD (2012), *Recommendation of the Council on Regulatory Policy and Governance*, OECD Publishing, Paris, https://dx.doi.org/10.1787/9789264209022-en. [1]

OECD (2009), *Regulatory Impact Analysis: A Tool for Policy Coherence*, OECD Reviews of Regulatory Reform, OECD Publishing, Paris, https://dx.doi.org/10.1787/9789264067110-en. [10]

OECD (2008), *Building an Institutional Framework for Regulatory Impact Analysis (RIA): Guidance for Policy Makers*, OECD Publishing, Paris, https://dx.doi.org/10.1787/9789264050013-en. [12]

OECD (2008), *Introductory Handbook for Undertaking Regulatory Impact Analysis (RIA)*, https://www.oecd.org/gov/regulatory-policy/44789472.pdf. [11]

OECD (2004), *Regulatory Impact Analysis (RIA) Inventory*, http://www.oecd.org/gov/regulatory-policy/35258430.pdf. [14]

OECD (1997), *Regulatory Impact Analysis: Best Practices in OECD Countries*, OECD Publishing, Paris, https://dx.doi.org/10.1787/9789264162150-en. [15]

Rodrigo, D. (2005), *Regulatory Impact Analysis in OECD Countries: Challenges for Developing Countries*, OECD, http://www.oecd.org/gov/regulatory-policy/35258511.pdf. [13]

2 Best practice principles for regulatory impact analysis

> **Box 2.1. Best practice principles for regulatory impact analysis**
>
> **1. Commitment and buy-in for RIA**
>
> - Governments should:
>   - Spell out what governments consider as "good regulations".
>   - Introduce RIA as part of a comprehensive long-term plan to boost the quality of regulation.
>   - Create an oversight unit for RIA with sufficient competences.
>   - Create credible "internal and external constraints", which guarantee that RIA will effectively be implemented.
>   - Secure political backing of RIA.
> - Securing stakeholder support is essential.
> - Governments have to ensure transparency of decision making to enable public control of the RIA process
>
> **2. Governance of RIA – having the right set up or system design**
>
> - RIA should be fully integrated with other regulatory management tools and should be implemented in the context of the Regulatory Governance Cycle.
> - RIA and its implementation should be adjusted to the legal and administrative system and culture of the country.
> - Governments need to decide whether to implement RIA at once or gradually.
> - Responsibilities for RIA programme elements have to be allocated carefully.
> - Efficient regulatory oversight is a crucial precondition for a successful RIA.
> - RIA should be proportional to the significance of the regulation. .
> - Parliaments should be encouraged to set up their own procedures to guarantee the quality of legislation, including the quality of RIA.
>
> **3. Embedding RIA through strengthening capacity and accountability of the administration.**
>
> - Adequate training must be provided to civil servants.
> - Governments should publish detailed guidance material.
> - There should be only limited exceptions to the general rule that RIA is required.
> - Accountability- and performance-oriented arrangements should be implemented.

4. Targeted and appropriate RIA methodology

- The RIA methodology should be as simple and flexible as possible, while ensuring certain key features are covered.
- RIA should not always be interpreted as requiring a full-fledged, quantitative cost-benefit analysis of legislation.
- Sound data governance strategies can help produce, collect, process, access and share data in the context of RIA.
- RIA has to follow all stages of the regulation-making process and has to start at the inception stage in order to inform policy development.
- No RIA can be successful without defining the policy context and objectives, in particular the systematic identification of the problem.
- All plausible alternatives, including non-regulatory solutions must be taken into account.
- It is essential to always identify all relevant direct and important indirect costs as well as benefits.
- Stakeholder engagement must be incorporated systematically in the RIA process.
- Insights from behavioural science and economics should be considered, as appropriate.
- The development of enforcement and compliance strategies should be part of every RIA.
- RIA should be perceived as an iterative process.
- Results of RIA should be well communicated.

5. Continuous monitoring, evaluation and improvement of RIA

- It is important to validate the real impacts of adopted regulations after their implementation.
- RIA systems should also have an in-built monitoring, evaluation and refinement mechanism in place. This includes early plans for data collection or access to data.
- A regular, comprehensive evaluation of the impact of RIA on the (perceived) quality of regulatory decisions is essential.
- It is important to evaluate the impacts in cases where the original RIA document does not coincide with the final text of the proposal
- Systematic evaluation of the performance of the regulatory oversight bodies is important.

As a minimum, every process of regulatory impact assessment should follow the steps summarised in Box 2.2. For RIA to be successful, it needs to have the following elements:

- RIA has to start at the inception stage in order to inform policy development ;
- Clearly identify the problem and desired goals of the proposal;
- Identify and evaluate all reasonable potential alternative solutions (including non-regulatory ones);
- Always attempt to assess all potential costs and benefits, both direct and indirect;
- Be based on the best reasonably obtainable evidence and scientific expertise;
- Be elaborated in consultations with stakeholders and well communicated.

> **Box 2.2. Basic steps in the regulatory impact assessment process**
>
> 1. Consultations and stakeholder engagement – Use inputs from all potentially affected stakeholders as well as other relevant experts in all stages of the RIA process.
> 2. Problem definition – Describe assessment of the nature and extent of the problem to be addressed by the regulatory proposal, preferably in quantitative terms.[1]
> 3. Objective – Clearly state the policy objective(s) and goal(s) of the regulatory proposal.
> 4. Description of the regulatory proposal – Describe the existing regulatory framework, the proposed draft, identify administrative bodies and institutions responsible for drafting, implementing and enforcing the proposal, outline the enforcement regime and proposed strategy for ensuring compliance.
> 5. Identification of alternatives – List the practical alternatives, including any non-regulatory approaches considered as potential solution of the identified problem.
> 6. Analysis of benefit and costs – Clearly outline the benefits and costs expected from alternatives identified in previous steps.
> 7. Identification of the preferred solution – Outline how and in what ways the identified regulatory proposal is superior to the alternatives that were considered.
> 8. Setting out the monitoring and evaluation framework – Describe how performance of the regulation will be evaluated and anticipate the necessary data requirements.
>
> Notes: RIA is an iterative process; therefore some of the steps might be performed repeatedly using inputs from the subsequent ones.
> 1. Qualitative terms might also be important, e.g. for public health issues.

The Principles are divided into the following five sections:

1. Commitment and buy-in for RIA;
2. Governance of RIA – having the right set up or system design;
3. Embedding RIA through strengthening capacity and accountability of the administration;
4. Targeted and appropriate RIA methodology; and
5. Continuous evaluation and improvement of RIA.

Commitment and buy-in for RIA

While RIA can be looked at as a "good policy-making process", naturally, there might be forces militating against its use, be it bureaucratic inertia, political need for speed, an appetite to adopt certain politically sensitive proposals without much scrutiny, etc. Therefore, it is necessary to create frameworks that will secure RIA in practice and will counter the efforts to avoid or undermine it, factoring in flexibility which should help facilitate buy-in from across government stakeholders. Political commitment has always been an important factor for RIA to be successfully integrated into regulatory policy. However, the type of commitment is also important in the relevant governance systems.

In addition to the support from inside the administration, a buy-in from stakeholders external to government creates a demand for good RIA. Activating key stakeholders that are in the private sector, civil society, media, and parliament not only creates demand for RIA but also provides mechanisms making policy makers and civil servants more accountable for their decisions to these stakeholders. This creates an incentive for political leadership, legislature and regulators to support RIA. Nurturing the "demand" for better regulation can help incorporating RIA in the regulatory policy cycle.

There are many ways in which governments can show their commitment towards RIA in the long run. To make sure this commitment and buy-in are sustainable, **governments should**:

- **Spell out what governments consider as "good regulations"** to which RIA should contribute. More generally, governments should explain that RIA is used to ensure that their regulation abides by the principles of necessity,[1] effectiveness,[2] proportionality,[3] predictability,[4] transparency,[5] accountability,[6] simplicity[7] and participation.[8]
- **Introduce RIA as part of a comprehensive long-term plan to boost the quality of regulation.** RIA alone will never be successful in improving the quality of regulation, unless coupled with additional regulatory reform tools such as the use of consultation, the adoption of a "policy cycle" approach with use of monitoring and *ex post* evaluation alongside with regular reviews of existing legislation (see also the forthcoming OECD Best Practice Principles on Stakeholder Engagement and on Reviewing the Stock of Regulation), etc.
- **Create an oversight unit for RIA with sufficient competences.** Preferably, depending on the governance system of a given country, the unit should be located close to the centre of government due to the horizontal nature of RIA. The level of political commitment for RIA is maximised whenever governments create an institutional setting that leads to an enhanced control over the development of the RIA system. This aspect is central to the effectiveness of RIA introduction, and is also related to the need for governments to "signal" their commitment to external stakeholders, and civil servants within the administration and other institutions (see also the following section).
- **Create credible "internal constraints"**. A commitment to RIA is more credible the more governments create internal procedural constraints that make RIA an (almost) inevitable requirement. Such internal constraints may include, for example:
    o a well-structured system of regulatory planning, which encourages administrations to start their work on regulatory proposals early enough that RIA can be accommodated in the regulatory process;
    o a requirement that all new (or at least major or those with significant impacts) regulatory proposals be coupled with a RIA document, to be presented in due time to gather comments from the oversight body;
    o the creation of dedicated RIA units for each department with sufficient analytical capacities, in charge of co-ordinating RIA work, with a clear incentive to promote the drafting of sound RIAs inside their administrations;
    o budgetary incentives related to compliance with RIA requirements, depending on the administrative system of a given country. This might even include limitation of budgetary resources to those administrative bodies systematically not complying with the obligation to conduct RIA.[9]

Create "external constraints", which guarantee that RIA will effectively be implemented. Constraints of external nature are also important to enhance the level of political commitment signalled to external stakeholders. The options for creating such constrains may include the following:

- a commitment to "open government", and in particular to a timely, sufficiently extended, fully open and participatory consultation process on major decisions;
- the publication of yearly reports based on clear indicators, which track the government's progress in implementing RIA;
- the creation of dedicated representation bodies in charge of representing specific external interests as attached to the administration, or external to it;[10]

- the adoption of specific "screens" in the RIA methodology, which ensure that governments will be considering specific impacts in all policies, and that failure to consider such interests could even be seen as grounds for corrective measures, potentially even invalidation of the legal text by administrative or constitutional courts, the Council of State, etc. (e.g. think small principle, consumer impacts, trade impact assessments, fundamental rights IA, etc.);[11]
- contemplating a role for other institutional bodies at arm's length of the government in the regular or ad hoc scrutiny of the quality of the RIA process, and/or in-depth analysis of the quality of individual RIAs;
- carrying out perception surveys on the government's ability to carry out high quality RIAs in support of better regulatory outcomes among civil servants, policy-makers and/or also external stakeholders.

Secure political backing of RIA. A key element that helps the consolidation of RIA and the credibility of government commitment towards regulatory reform is the stability of the reforms proposed. This is why securing bipartisan (or "multi-party", depending on the level of fragmentation of the political landscape) consensus is fundamental to regulatory reform. Possible ways to achieve such a widespread endorsement could be, for example, the following:[12]

- seeking the broadest possible political agreement on the proposed regulatory reform plan as well as on the RIA methodology;
- appointing an independent oversight body or a parliamentary committee on regulatory reform,[13]
- introducing the requirement for RIA in primary legislation (or even the country's constitution[14]) as a general rule that will apply to the regulatory process for the coming generations.

Securing stakeholder support is essential not only as a way to create consensus on a given better regulation strategy and secure support by key constituencies over time. In most of the countries that have successfully introduced RIA, the centre-of-government has managed to convince bureaucrats of the need to draft high quality RIAs also by creating expectations among, and a constant dialogue with, external stakeholders. Importantly, publicity of RIA and adequate consultation of RIA drafts can also increase the quality of the debate and of the final RIA document, and stimulate the birth and development of think tanks, industry and consumer associations, who need to strengthen their ability to respond quickly to government consultations.

Governments have to ensure transparency of decision making to enable public control of the RIA process. Consultation on the draft RIA document is particularly useful since it can focus on the structure of the document, the data used, the alternative options selected, the criteria applied for comparing options, and the overall quality of the analysis adopted to select a specific preferred policy option. It is, in other words, a technical consultation process, rather than a political one (which focuses on the substance of the regulation and can be carried out later or at the same time), and as such can help administrations collect valuable information and avoid macroscopic mistakes from the outset.

Governance of RIA – having the right set up or system design

Apart from building consensus around the introduction of RIA by showing political commitment and securing backing from stakeholders and public officials, another key element in the design of a successful RIA system is governance. Making the right choices with respect to a number of governance-related aspects is essential to trigger virtuous dynamics and sufficient incentives inside government.

RIA should be fully integrated with other regulatory management tools and should be implemented in the context of the Regulatory Governance Cycle.[15] A responsive administration performs an *ex ante* RIA, but also provides for monitoring, data collection and evaluation indicators and an *ex post* evaluation, which itself leads to the identification of the need for further action and a new *ex ante* assessment phase.

The evaluation of existing regulations should always take part before launching the development of new ones. Awareness of the entirety of the policy cycle is very important for a government that considers the introduction of RIA. Successful implementation of RIA is not possible without a functioning legislation planning system. Also, the implementation and enforcement phase should be taken into account already during the RIA process (which institution will be responsible for enforcing the regulation, how will regulated subjects be informed, etc.). RIA should also be coordinated with other potential assessment processes (e.g. policy costing or spending reviews done as part of the budget process). RIA should make use, where relevant, of existing data and evaluation indicators – e.g., for countries monitoring performance indicators as part of the budget process, those collected by Ministries of Finance and audited by the Supreme Audit Institution.

RIA and its implementation should be adjusted to the legal and administrative system and culture of the country, e.g. the level of skills and resources, the location of skills within (or outside) the administration, the level of consensus among external stakeholders, the existence of a culture of open government within the administration and among stakeholders. There are countless paths towards the establishment of a successful RIA system: as diverse as RIA systems are, even more diverse are the paths to each of the variants of RIA available on a global scale. Nevertheless, the ultimate goal should always be a full-fledge RIA framework implemented through improvements over time, especially in terms of resources and skills inside the administration.

Governments need to decide whether to implement RIA at once or gradually. Given the limited resources and experience with RIA, gradual implementation might be advisable for most countries. When RIA is being implemented, it is desirable to develop an implementation plan with measurable goals. Once the basic preconditions are met or at least planned, there are different possible paths to the gradual introduction of RIA, as described below:

- A pilot phase, then the institutionalisation of RIA for all or all major regulations;
- Starting with a simplified methodology, and then expand;
- Starting from some institutions, and then expand RIA to others;
- Starting from major regulatory proposals, and then lower the threshold to cover less significant regulations;
- Starting with binding regulation and then moving to soft-law;
- Starting with single- or multi-criteria qualitative analysis, and then gradually moving to quantitative analysis (CBA or other);
- From concentrated RIA expertise to more distributed responsibilities.

Responsibilities for RIA programme elements have to be allocated carefully. Since government bodies develop regulatory proposals, these institutions should also be responsible for the preparation of RIA. While some countries have relied on external consultants to carry out some of the components of the start-up phase, e.g. pilot projects or initial steps, it is important that the country develops a core team that has a "cross-functional" nature,[16] i.e. involving individuals with different backgrounds and skills. Creating inter-disciplinary (including inter-ministerial) groups where possible is essential for RIA to be balanced and drafted by people with a diverse range of expertise. Appointing sub-units with RIA expertise within relevant ministries or departments can prove essential, as it concentrates the need for advanced skills in the hands of a few experts per administration. This, in turn, requires that a strong oversight body is able to challenge the conclusions these experts have reached.

Effective regulatory oversight is a crucial precondition for a successful RIA. The Recommendation of the Council on Regulatory Policy and Governance recommends creating the oversight body "close to the centre of government, to ensure that regulation serves whole-of-government policy"; to set forth its authority in mandate, such as statute or executive order, and to make it independent from political influence when exercising its mandate. Depending on the legal and administrative system, the administration has to decide whether to locate the oversight body inside or outside the government and where inside the government administration. However, the body should be independent from the one developing the draft regulation being assessed. The oversight body needs to be given a consistent mandate which must be accompanied by suitable instruments.

RIA should be proportional to the significance of the regulation. RIA must be carefully/proportionately targeted in line with the size of the regulatory impact. Policy makers should target RIA towards regulatory proposals that are expected to have the largest impact on society, and ensure that all such proposals be subject to RIA scrutiny. The depth of the analysis should depend on the significance of the regulation being analysed. RIA, if carried out properly, takes time and resources. To ensure the right focus of the RIA framework, it is advisable to focus on the most important and impactful regulatory measures. Not all legislative proposals should go through the same level of analysis. Possible alternatives for sorting out which legislative proposals have to go through a certain level of analysis are:

- setting quantitative thresholds (e.g. potential impacts over 100 mil. USD in the USA);
- introducing a set of criteria (on issues such as the extent of the impact on competition, market openness, employment, productivity, innovation, investment as well the number of people affected by the proposed regulation.),
- multi-criteria analysis[17] or
- a general principle of proportionate analysis (such as the one used by the European Commission). The choice of how deep should the RIA can be left to the administration itself, based on a principle of proportionality. At the same time, such choice requires the scrutiny of an oversight body able to intervene and suggest a deeper analysis in case the proportionality principle has not been applied.

It is very important that the application of the threshold is transparent, and that the results of the application of the threshold are publicly shared. In addition, the role of regulatory oversight in ensuring that RIA is focusing on the most significant regulations is crucial.

Many countries are using different stages of RIA ("small"/preliminary, vs. „big" RIA). A two-step approach involves a preliminary RIA to identify regulations which should be subject to a detailed RIA. In such cases, a filter would be applied to most regulatory proposals, and a full RIA undertaken only for certain proposals, on the basis of defined thresholds. The fact that a regulation is required for compliance with international standards or supranational regulations is in some countries taken as a factor for deciding that a detailed RIA should not be applied. This might be dangerous as such regulations might have significant regulatory impacts and there still might be some "marge de manoeuvre" in terms of detailed implementation impact of which still has to be analysed. Other criteria for conducting a full RIA could be potential impacts on the competitiveness of the economy or a disproportionate impact on a sector or a group of stakeholders.

Parliaments should be encouraged to set up their own procedures to guarantee the quality of legislation, including the quality of RIA. As the institutions responsible for approving legislation, parliaments can exercise oversight and control over the application of better regulation principles for new and amended regulation. Parliaments should actively use and the government RIAs and checks their completeness and, if possible, quality. Indeed, regulatory practices cannot be "cut and pasted" from the executive and need to be carefully designed to fit into the legislative setting.

Embedding RIA through strengthening capacity and accountability of the administration

Embedding RIA into the existing policy-making and decision-making processes is important. When RIA is a "stand alone" initiative it is not integral to the regulatory policy cycle and as such has limited if any effect on regulatory design/outcomes/societal welfare. RIA should be connected to the machinery government and the decision-making body of government, such as the cabinet or council of Ministers.

Governments must be aware of the fact and explain to stakeholders that RIA and better regulation are a medium- to long-term investment for the quality of regulation and of the political debate in a country: rather than being a panacea that solves all problems within a short timeframe, RIA and related better regulation tools such as *ex post* evaluation can trigger a learning process that will improve legislation over time, with the help of all stakeholders.

Adequate training must be provided to civil servants that will potentially be charged with the drafting of RIA documents, as well as to understanding it and using it in their daily activities. Therefore, the training should, besides techniques for problem definition, setting policy objectives, identifying alternative solution, impact assessment, stakeholder engagement, and implementation of RIA, focus on real-life practical examples and case studies. Pilot projects can be used to make RIA training more targeted and relevant, which helps secure buy-in of the regulators who are to implement RIA. These can range from the large-scale rolling out of RIA in selected government departments to very small-scale, half-day workshops to discuss a particular RIA with policy-makers and stakeholders. (Adelle et al., 2015[1]) Competent and committed public officials have shown to be a key ingredient of a successful RIA system, convincing them on the usefulness of RIA is therefore crucial. Skills are essential for RIA: knowing how to draft and also how to read a RIA document is a very challenging activity, which requires good expertise and the ability to communicate and trigger adequate learning. At the same time, training should not become just a one-off experience: training will only become useful to motivate civil servants if they know they will be rewarded with their ability to master RIA in their daily work.

Governments should publish detailed guidance material, typically covering both the procedural requirements associated with RIA and the substantive aspects of RIA preparation. In addition, guidance on various analytical techniques should be made available. Given the technical nature of these techniques (such as CBA), general RIA guidance documents sometimes refer readers to separate, more detailed guidance documents. More recently, a number of countries have developed software-based tools that can be used to assist in RIA development.[18] These calculators are, in some countries, accessible also to stakeholders, which can calculate the costs of current, drafted or potential regulations or their changes.

There should be only limited exceptions to the general rule that RIA is required.[19] Legitimate cases for exemptions (e.g. budget laws, national security matters) and exceptions (e.g. emergencies, market sensitive issues) from the RIA requirement exist. Nevertheless, too many exceptions to the obligation to perform RIA can become an alibi for administrations, whose role could become that of looking for the best excuse to put forward for not carrying out the analysis.

Accountability- and performance-oriented arrangements should be implemented in accordance with the legal and administrative system of a given country. These could include, for example:

- specifying the name of the responsible person for every regulatory proposal that is tabled by government and published online;
- sign-off of RIA statements by responsible ministers/high-level officials/heads of administrative authorities;
- including the evaluation of RIA work as an element in the evaluation of the performance and the determination of productivity of the civil servant;
- specifying that skills in RIA are an element to be considered for career promotion to specific high-responsibility positions in the administration.

Targeted and appropriate RIA methodology

It is often said that there is no "one size fits all" for applying RIA. This may also be relevant for the RIA methodology. Cost-Benefit Analysis (CBA) is one methodology that has been applied successfully but the complexity of the methodology varies across countries and even within countries. Other methodologies include comparing positive and negative impacts, qualitative and quantitative methods, multi-criteria analysis, partial and general equilibrium analysis, as well as assessing direct and indirect effects. The RIA methodology must first suit the objective of RIA as well as the administrative context and capacity.

The RIA methodology should be as simple and flexible as possible, while ensuring certain key features are covered. This is particularly the case when in "start-up" mode. Being able to adapt to the needs of decision-makers is key to maintaining the relevance of RIA. It can also address one of the main barriers to RIA implementation, which is the public official perception of RIA as being overwhelming and unrealistic. The examples could include not always requiring full-fledged CBA (see below), not requiring quantification if data are objectively not available, etc.

RIA should not always be interpreted as requiring a full-fledged, quantitative cost-benefit analysis of legislation. A full assessment of macroeconomic impacts necessarily requires the adoption of sophisticated economic modelling. It is unlikely to be feasible in the majority of cases, given the general scarcity of expertise and resources available for the conduct of RIA in most countries. In such circumstances, implementing requirements to undertake substantially more demanding analyses involving general equilibrium models risks having perverse impacts, by diverting resources and focus from more feasible RIA tasks. Various methodologies can be used to compare positive and negative impacts of regulation, including qualitative and quantitative methods, cost-benefit analysis and multi-criteria methods, partial and general equilibrium analyses. Rather than always engaging in quantitative cost-benefit analysis, it is essential that officials in charge of RIA identify all possible direct and indirect impacts of alternative options that can in principle address and solve the identified policy problem. (See Box 2.3 for examples of various possible methods). Still, the goal of the administration implementing RIA should lie in making cost-benefit analysis integral to a RIA.

Box 2.3. Choosing the right methodology: Towards more sophisticated RIA methods?

One of the key challenges in performing RIA is the choice of the most appropriate methodology to assess the impacts and compare alternative regulatory options. A first important choice to be made is the choice of whether to perform a partial equilibrium analysis or a general equilibrium analysis. The latter typically requires modelling abilities, and as such can and should be chosen only when a number of specific conditions are met: in particular, indirect impacts have to appear significant, and spread across various sectors of the economy; in addition, there must be sufficient skills within the administration, or the possibility to commission a general equilibrium modelling analysis from a high-quality, reliable group of researchers inside or outside the administration. General equilibrium analysis is preferred by many scholars for its ability to capture very dispersed indirect impacts of regulation. For the time being, however, it is likely that the overwhelming majority of administrations will continue to use partial equilibrium analysis in RIA. However, where a regulation will materially affect one or more closely related markets or will have diverse and far reaching effects across the economy, a general equilibrium framework is required to assess these impacts.

When performing partial equilibrium analysis, typically the methodological choices available to administrations are the following:

- Least cost analysis looks only at costs, in order to select the alternative option that entails the lowest cost. This method is typically chosen whenever benefits are fixed, and the administrations only needs to choose how to achieve them.
- Cost-effectiveness analysis (CEA) entails that administrations quantify (not monetise) the benefits that would be generated by one USD of costs imposed on society. The typical method used to compare options is thus the so-called benefit-cost ratio, which means dividing the benefits by costs. This method is normally used to all expenditure programs, as it leads to identifying the "value for money" of various expenditure programs. A typical question that can

> be answered through cost-effectiveness analysis is "how many jobs will be created for every Dollar invested in this option?"; or, "how many lives are saved by every Euro spent on this option?".
> - Cost-benefit analysis (CBA) entails the monetisation of all (or the most important) costs and benefits related to all viable alternatives at hand. In its most recurrent form, it disregards distributional impacts and only focuses on the selection of the regulatory alternative that exhibits the highest societal net benefit. Accordingly, the most common methodology in cost-benefit analysis is the "net benefits" calculation, which differs from the "benefit/cost ratio" method that is typically used in cost-effectiveness analysis (being benefit minus costs, rather than benefits divided by costs).
> - Multi-criteria analysis allows a comparison of alternative policy options along a set of pre-determined criteria. For example, criteria chosen could include the impact on SMEs, the degree of protection of fundamental rights, consumer protection, etc. Multi-Criteria Analysis is particularly useful when Impact Assessment has to be reconciled with specific policy objectives, and as such is used as an instrument of policy coherence. This method is more likely to capture distributional impacts, although this crucially depends on the criteria chosen for evaluating options.
>
> Source: (OECD, 2015[2]), "Regulatory Impact Assessment and regulatory policy", in Regulatory Policy in Perspective: A Reader's Companion to the OECD Regulatory Policy Outlook 2015, OECD Publishing, Paris, https://doi.org/10.1787/9789264241800-5-en.

Sound data governance strategies can help in building the right foundations to **produce, collect, process, access and sharing data in the context of RIA.** Delivering value implies stressing the importance of evidence-based policymaking. In this light, tapping the value of data and new technologies (e.g. big data, AI) can help in better design, deploy, monitor and evaluate the impact of policy and regulation (OECD, 2019[3]). This implies involving relevant data holders and all potential sources of unbiased data (academics, institutes of statistics, etc.) in order to ensure that those data helps governments take the best possible course of action, based on the most complete and reliable information set. For instance, as discussed in the 2019 OECD Report *The Path to Becoming a Data-Driven Public Sector* (OECD, 2019[3]), OECD countries are increasingly benefiting from deploying shared data governance frameworks in the context of their regulatory activity (see Box 2.4). This helps is ensuring the enhanced access to and sharing of data (EASD) for a meaningful problem definition, for a careful analysis of the alternative solutions available, and also for an estimate of the compliance and enforcement costs associated with each of the alternative policy options. Increasingly involving statistical institutes and other relevant data holders within and outside the public sector is crucial to ensure streamlined data management and real-time data processing practices that can help in ensuring the access to trustworthy data sources informing RIA. For instance, complete and constantly evolving data on the performance of existing legislation, on the perception of citizens and industry, on the quality of existing rules, and on the potential impact of exogenous factors in the short- to medium-term. The potential of using and processing big data for developing better regulations is currently examined by many countries and should be fully exploited in the future.

> **Box 2.4. Netherlands: Promoting shared data governance frameworks in the context of regulatory compliance**
>
> The definition of a common data governance framework (from regulations to data federation tools and standards) in the context of regulatory activity can help in promoting data integration; and increase the adoption of good data management practices. The OECD model for public sector data governance (see Figure 2.1) highlights a set of elements and components that can help governments, line ministries, agencies and public sector organisations to deploy data sharing and access practices that can be fostered by the application of new technologies and tools (e.g. big data, linked data, APIs). The model is scalable for its replicability and can be applied to data sharing and access practices across organisations, levels of government, policy areas, sectors and borders.
>
> **Figure 2.1. Data governance in the public sector**
>
>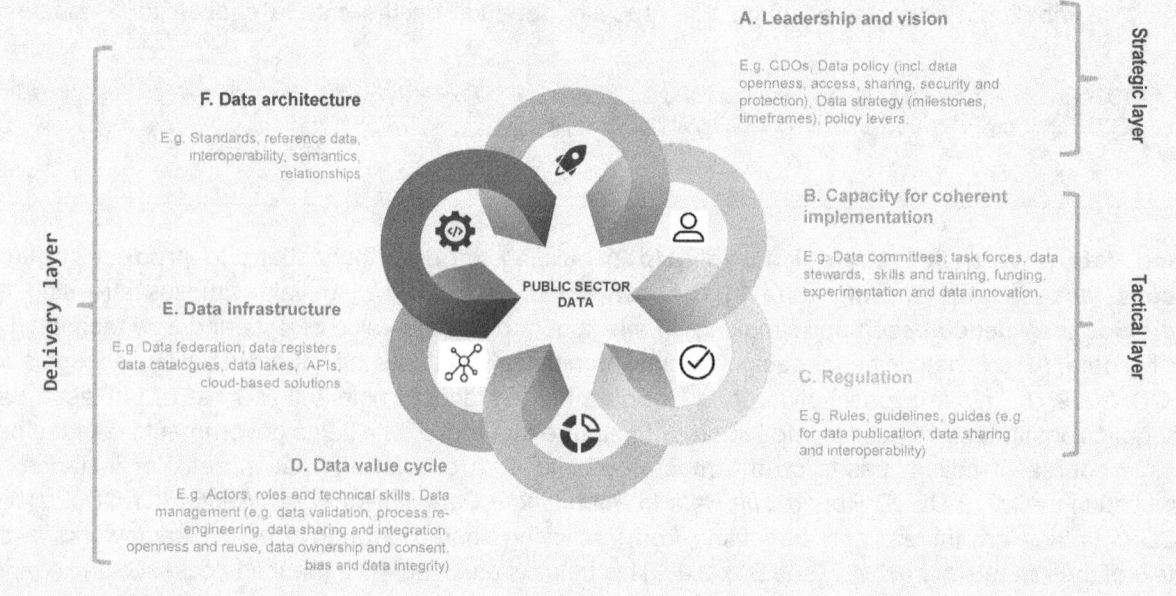
>
> Source: OECD (2019[3]), The Path to Becoming a Data-Driven Public Sector, Paris, https://dx.doi.org/10.1787/059814a7-en.

If the benefits to policy are to be realised, **RIA has to follow all stages of the regulation-making process and has to start at the inception stage of policy development**, when there is a genuine interest in identifying the best available solution and there is an opportunity to consider alternatives to regulation. It is only if RIA is commenced at an early stage of policy development that there is any real possibility of it being adopted as an integral part of the policy process, rather than as a separate, procedurally-based requirement which takes on the character of an *ex post* rationalisation of the policy choice already made.

No RIA can be successful without defining the policy context and objectives, in particular the systematic identification of the problem that provides the basis for action by government. In evaluating the RIA's expressed need for regulatory action, administrations should be wary of anecdotal observations that may illustrate symptoms of a problem without articulating the underlying cause of those symptoms. Regulatory actions that do not explicitly point to a failure of private markets or public institutions underlying the need for action are likely to produce lower net benefits than those that correctly identify and seek to remedy the fundamental problem. (Dudley et al., 2017[4]) Poor problem identification might lead to unjustified regulations and difficulties in monitoring and assessing the effectiveness and efficiency of these regulations.

All plausible alternatives, including non-regulatory solutions must be taken into account. A "do-nothing option" – the assumed state of the world in the absence of the regulation (the "counterfactual," or "baseline") should always be included. RIAs should examine human welfare differences among alternative policies. Thus, it is important to look at whether the RIA considers plausible alternatives or if it only presents the preferred regulatory approach (perhaps with some unrealistic straw men alternatives). Do alternatives vary in their stringency? Are different regulatory instruments considered? Is evidence presented that allows you to easily evaluate alternatives and their relative effect on human welfare? Or does the RIA seem to focus on justifying a particular regulatory action? (Dudley et al., 2017[4]) For a typology of alternatives to "command-and-control" regulations see Box 2.5

Box 2.5. Alternatives to "command-and-control" regulations

Performance-based regulations: Performance-based regulation specifies required outcomes or objectives, rather than the means by which they must be achieved. Firms and individuals are able to choose the process by which they will comply with the law. This allows them to identify processes that are more efficient and lower cost in relation to their circumstances, and also promotes innovation and the adoption of new technology on a broader scale.

Process-based regulations: These regulations are so named because they require businesses to develop processes that ensure a systematic approach to controlling and minimising production risks. They are based on the idea that, given the right incentives, producers are likely to prove more effective in identifying hazards and developing lowest-cost solutions than is a central regulatory authority. They are particularly useful where there are multiple and complex sources of risk, and *ex post* testing of the product is either relatively ineffective or prohibitively expensive.

Co-regulation: Under co-regulation, the regulatory role is shared between government and industry. It is usually effected through legislative reference or endorsement of a code of practice. Typically, the industry or a large proportion of industry participants formulate a code of practice in consultation with government, with breaches of the code usually enforceable via sanctions imposed by industry or professional organisations rather than the government directly. This approach allows industry to take the lead in the regulation of its members by setting standards and encouraging greater responsibility for performance. It also exploits the expertise and knowledge held within the industry or professional association.

Economic regulation: A more modern explanation sees economic regulation being less about correcting for market failures and more about enabling markets to work more effectively. That is, where the disciplines of competition are weak or absent, an economic regulator acts as a 'visible hand' seeking to guide service providers towards outcomes (e.g. in terms of price, quality or both) that would have occurred had the market been subject to those competitive disciplines.

Economic instruments: At a theoretical level, the use of economic instruments should a priori be the preferred means of achieving policy objectives in a wide range of situations. This is because these tools – taxes, subsidies, tradable permits, vouchers and the like – operate directly through the market, thus harnessing market incentives and avoiding the substantial potential for distorting market incentives inherent in most forms of regulation.

Information and education: The most widely used alternative approach to regulation in OECD member countries is information and education campaigns. These approaches address information asymmetries and empower citizens and consumers to adopt actions or make informed choices that

> match their preferences and align their sensibility to risks. While many information campaigns simply seek to inform citizens and enhance consumer choice, some information campaigns are more explicit in seeking to change behaviour.
>
> **Voluntary approaches:** Voluntary approaches are arrangements initiated and undertaken by industry and firms, sometimes formally sanctioned or endorsed by government, in which self-imposed requirements which go beyond or complement the prevailing regulatory requirements. They include voluntary initiatives, voluntary codes, voluntary agreements, and self-regulation and can vary in regard to their enforceability and degree of voluntarism.
>
> **Behavioural insights (BI):** Uses an inductive approach to policy making that seeks to understand how context and biases influence decision-making, and pre-test solutions to determine what works before implementing at larger scale. This method uses insights from psychology, cognitive science, and social science to anticipate the behavioural consequences of policies and ultimately design and deliver more effective policies by using behaviourally-informed strategies to guide decision making.
>
> Source: (OECD, 2002[5]), OECD Reviews of Regulatory Reform: Regulatory Policies in OECD Countries, Paris, https://dx.doi.org/10.1787/9789264177437-en; https://www.esc.vic.gov.au/sites/default/files/documents/What-Is-Economic-Regulation.pdf; (OECD, 2019[6]), Tools and Ethics for Applied Behavioural Insights: The BASIC Toolkit, OECD Publishing, Paris, https://doi.org/10.1787/9ea76a8f-en.

It is essential to always identify all relevant direct and important indirect costs as well as benefits that would emerge if the available regulatory options are implemented. This can enable a more meaningful comparison of regulatory options. Regardless of whether RIA is eventually based on CBA or not, identifying all groups of stakeholders who would be impacted and how they will be impacted, as well as potential disproportionalities in these impacts can enable a more meaningful comparison of regulatory options. It is necessary to go beyond direct economic impacts and include various types of impacts, such as impacts on environment (see for example (OECD, 2018[7])), social impacts (jobs, public health, gender equality, poverty, inequalities and their reduction, working conditions, etc.), impacts on innovation, cross-border impacts and also second-round effects and unintended consequences, etc. RIA should also take into account the Sustainable Development Goals. Wherever partial impact assessments are being conducted separately, they should be integrated into one crosscutting integrated impact assessment. For a taxonomy of compliance costs see Figure 2.2, for a methodology on measuring compliance costs see (OECD, 2014[8]). Given that SMEs represent the largest share of companies in most economies, SME-friendly legislation is an important pre-conditions for a favourable business environment. Many countries adopted an approach similar to the "think small first" principle which requires public authorities to take into consideration the interests and needs of SMEs at an early stage of policy making. RIA mechanisms should explicitly consider the impact of the legislation on SMEs (the "SME test") as an integral part of the assessment. The SME test may lead to the exclusion of SMEs (often micro-enterprises) from the scope of regulations, or to the introduction of exemptions, transition periods or tailor-made provisions for SMEs.

Figure 2.2. Taxonomy of regulatory costs

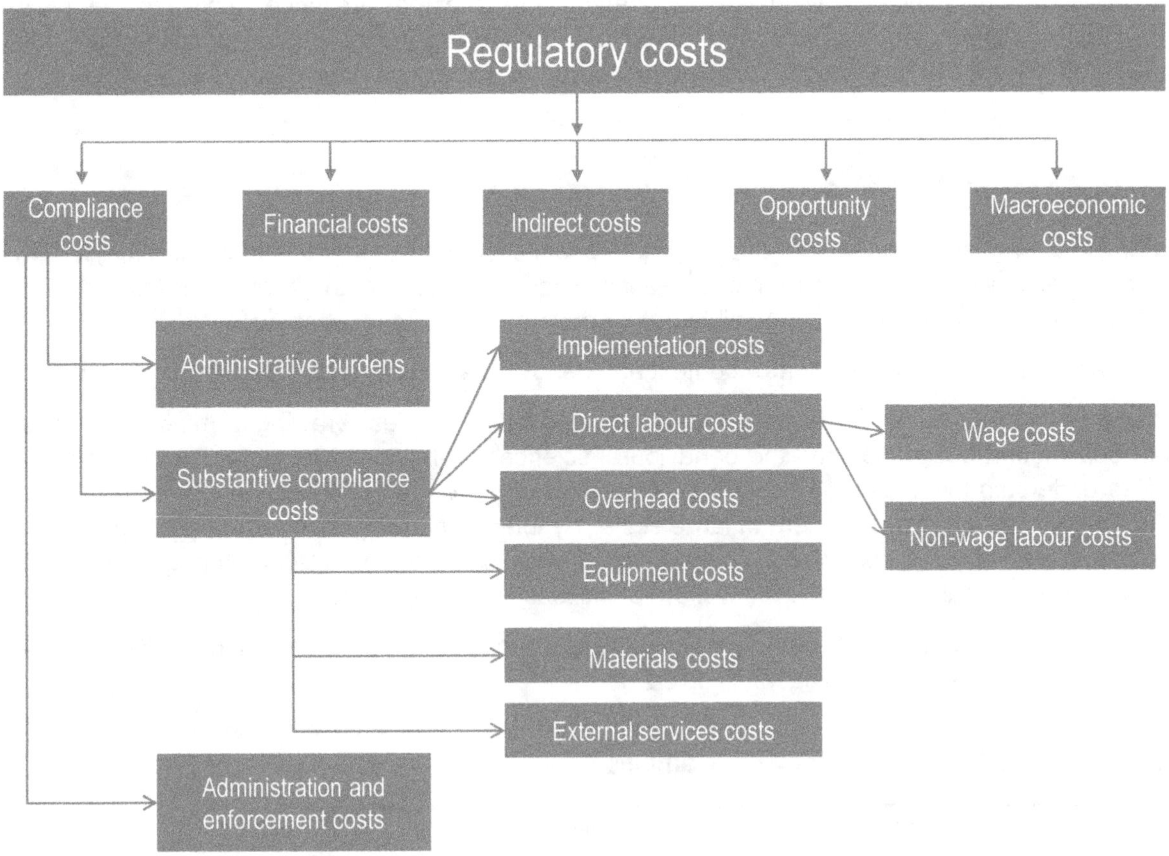

```
                              Regulatory costs
    ┌──────────────┬──────────────┬──────────────┬──────────────┐
Compliance    Financial     Indirect      Opportunity   Macroeconomic
  costs         costs        costs          costs           costs
    │
    ├─► Administrative burdens        ─► Implementation costs
    │                                 ─► Direct labour costs ──► Wage costs
    ├─► Substantive compliance        ─► Overhead costs
    │   costs                         ─► Equipment costs     ─► Non-wage labour costs
    │                                 ─► Materials costs
    │                                 ─► External services costs
    └─► Administration and
        enforcement costs
```

Source: (OECD, 2014[8]), *OECD Regulatory Compliance Cost Assessment Guidance*, Paris, http://dx.doi.org/10.1787/9789264209657-en.

Stakeholder engagement must be incorporated systematically in the RIA process to give an opportunity for all stakeholders to participate in the regulatory process. Stakeholders might provide important information on the costs and benefits of alternatives, including their effectiveness. An example of an innovative tool that can help in making RIA more open and participatory is the publication of open and linked data on draft regulations, or other segments of the regulatory process, making it easier for stakeholders to participate in the regulatory process, and monitor and assist in shaping better regulations. The public, especially those affected by regulations, can also themselves often provide much of the data needed to complete the RIA. Consultation and user engagement can furnish important information on the feasibility of proposals, on the alternatives considered, and on the degree to which affected parties are likely to comply with the proposed regulation. Furthermore, the assumptions and data used in RIA can also be improved if they are tested after the carrying out of the RIA through public disclosure and consultation. Some form of guidance for stakeholder engagement on the ways of engagement, handling data, topic for consultations and mechanisms to submit comments as well as on the way of providing feedback to stakeholders is advisable (see also the forthcoming *OECD Best Practice Principles on Stakeholder Engagement and Regulatory Policy*).

Insights from behavioural science and economics should be considered, as appropriate. Policy issues often contain both structural (i.e. legal, economic incentives, technical, etc.) and behavioural (i.e. errors in decision making based on context and biases) drivers. Omitting a behavioural analysis of a policy problem can lead to a misunderstanding of the problem itself, and miss an opportunity to incorporate behaviourally-informed solutions that can lead to more effective policy outcomes. Broadly, behavioural drivers of policy problems can be categorised according to four key drivers: attention, belief formation, choices and determination – or "ABCD" (Box 2.6). This extends to organisational decision making, as organisations are made up of individuals and evidence shows that they are influenced via the people inside them. OECD (2019[6]) provides policymakers with a toolkit and set of ethical guidelines for applying behavioural insights (BI) to any policy problem from start to finish.

> ### Box 2.6. The "ABCD" of behavioural insights in public policy
>
> Have you ever missed an important appointment because you had too much to do and forgot? Given up on properly filling out a public form because it was too cumbersome and hard to understand? Driven a little above the speed limit because all the other drivers were going fast as well?
>
> These are everyday examples of how context and behavioural biases can influence decision-making.
>
> A better understanding of human behaviour can lead to better policies. Drawing from rigorous research from behavioural economics and the behavioural sciences, behavioural insights (BI) can help public bodies understand why citizens behave as they do and pretest which policy solutions are the most effective before implementing them at large scale. By integrating BI into policy making, policy makers can better anticipate the behavioural consequences of policies and ultimately design and deliver more effective policies that can improve the welfare of citizens.
>
> The "ABCD" framework focuses on four key drivers of behavioural policy problems: Attention, Belief Formation, Choice and Determination (Table 2.1):
>
> #### Table 2.1. The ABCD framework with examples
>
> | The ABCD of behavioural drivers | Sample policy problem | Behavioural strategy | Impact |
> |---|---|---|---|
> | **Attention:** people's attention is limited and easily distracted | Patients fail to attend their medical appointments | Send SMS reminders that include the cost of a missed appointment to the health system | 25% reduction in missed appointments |
> | **Belief formation:** people rely on mental shortcuts and often over/under estimate outcomes and probabilities | Residents speed up at sharp turns, resulting in more car crashes | Paint a series of white lines to create the illusion of speeding up so people slow down | 36% fewer crashes in 6 months |
> | **Choice:** People are influenced by the framing and the social as well as situation contexts of choices | Households do not make sufficient efforts for energy efficiency | Send letters to utility customers comparing their electricity consumption to that of neighbours | 2.0% reduction in electricity consumption, resulting in a reduction of 450k tonnes of CO_2 and USD 75 million in savings |
> | **Determination:** Even when people make good choices, people's willpower is limited and subject to psychological biases that prevent long-run success | Job seekers are struggling to find work | Create a "commitment pack" that includes meeting with an employment advisor to create an actionable job-hunting plan | 23% more job seekers found work |
>
> Source: (OECD, 2019[6]), Tools and Ethics for Applied Behavioural Insights: The BASIC Toolkit, Paris, https://doi.org/10.1787/9ea76a8f-en.

The development of implementation, enforcement and compliance strategies for each option, including an evaluation of their effectiveness and efficiency **should be part of every RIA**. It is important, already at the stage of drafting regulations, to develop a realistic, practical and co-ordinated plan for the implementation of the selected measure. RIA should clearly state which institution(s) will be responsible for implementing and enforcing the regulation and also what resources will be needed and how they will be made available. In designing the implementation strategy, RIA should also consider alternatives to state-led regulatory enforcement (such as market forces, private sector and civil society actions). When considering whether state-led regulatory enforcement is truly required, it is important to consider the question of compliance incentives. (For more information, see (OECD, 2014[9]).

RIA should be perceived as an iterative process of considering and evaluating policy alternatives that contributes to improving the policy capacities of the administration to make better decisions rather than a magic formula which automatically generates the best solution to every problem. In essence, RIA attempts to widen and clarify the relevant factors for decision-making. It implicitly broadens the mission of regulators from highly-focused problem-solving to balanced decisions that trade off problems against wider economic and distributional goals. Far from being a technocratic tool that can be simply "added on" to the decision-making system by policy directive, it is a method for transforming the view of what is appropriate action. Once this is clearly understood, it is easier to appreciate the long-term perspective for a RIA and its role in the policy decision process.

Results of RIA should be well communicated. RIAs should not be written in a way that obfuscates important information or skews the analysis to support a particular outcome (Dudley et al., 2017[4]). RIA communication should also respect certain prerequisites of information established by regulatory authorities but maintain a reasonable level of simplicity and conciseness. To complete the publication, references should be made available in annexes to allow interested users to find the background information used to undertake the RIA and inform about the robustness of the evidence base, assumptions and their limitations, etc. Preferably, each RIA statement should include a short, easy-to-understand summary, e.g. in a form of the table, briefly introducing the assessed options, their costs and benefits and justifying why the preferred option has been selected.

Continuous monitoring, evaluation and improvement of RIA

The scope of the analysis should be expanded to cover the policy cycle. **It is important to validate the real impacts of adopted regulations** sometime **after their implementation**. This will not only help to improve the quality of regulations themselves but also inform future *ex ante* RIAs by gathering data and providing feedback on the RIA development process. To be able to do this, appropriate data on impacts of regulations must be collected drawing upon the deployment of sound data governance and management practices from the beginning (see previous section), which can enhance data trustworthiness and accuracy. Recognising the relevance of the Government Data Value Cycle (see Box 2.7) throughout the policy and regulatory cycle means data requirements will be considered from the outset during the regulatory development phase. By focussing on data requirements at an earlier stage in regulatory design, we can more clearly articulate how the achievement of regulatory goals will be measured. Data which reflect regulatory outcomes, rather than inputs or outputs, need to be collected. *Ex post* impact analysis is also very important in cases of regulations adopted with an exception from going through *ex ante* RIA, for example in cases of emergency.

Box 2.7. Managing and applying data to generate public value

The Government Data Value Cycle identifies the stages through which data pass in order to be managed well. The cycle tracks the journey from handling data (raw, isolated and unstructured datasets) to identifying and understanding the relationships between those data, resulting in information and knowledge that form the basis for governments to take action and make decisions. This happens through feedback loops and ongoing iteration with data informing and affecting the nature of decision-making processes, which in turn lead to the production and collection of different or more data.

Figure 2.3. The Government Data Value Cycle

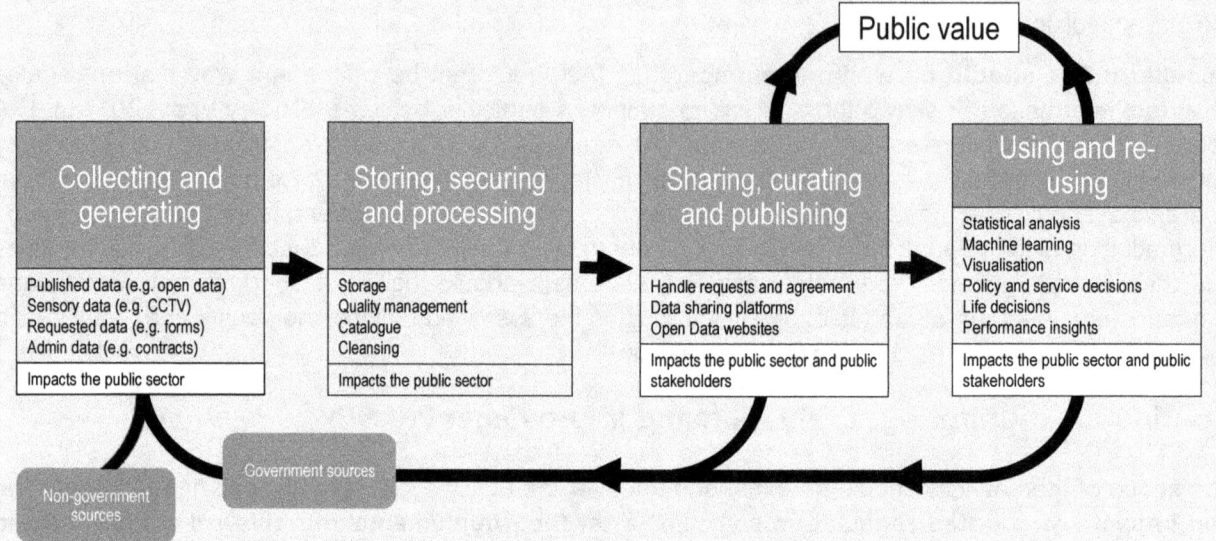

Source: (OECD, 2019[18]), The path to becoming a data-driven public sector, Paris, https://dx.doi.org/10.1787/059814a7-en.

RIA activities benefit from the governance and management of data according to that cycle but there are also opportunities in terms of applying data to generate public value. Considering the flow of data from planning, through delivery and into monitoring is particularly relevant for *ex post* RIA evaluation.

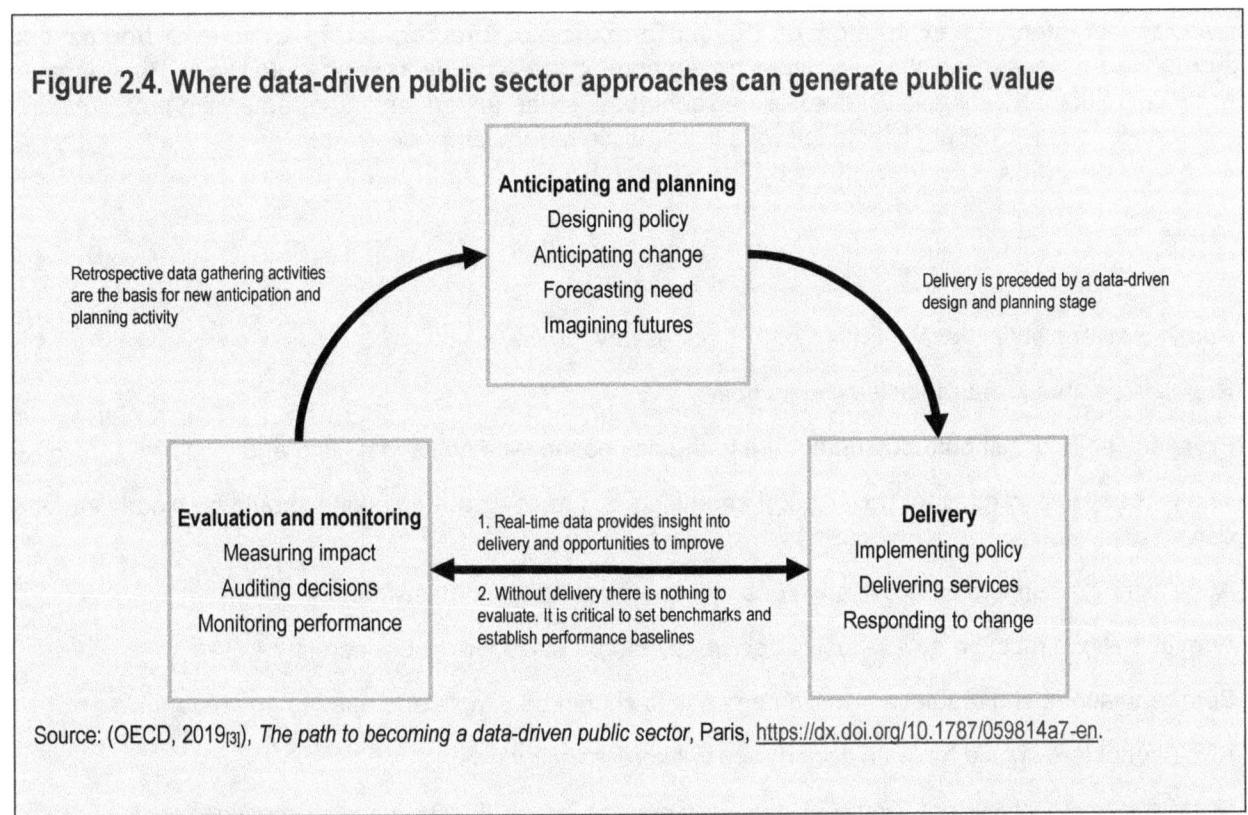
Figure 2.4. Where data-driven public sector approaches can generate public value

Source: (OECD, 2019[3]), *The path to becoming a data-driven public sector*, Paris, https://dx.doi.org/10.1787/059814a7-en.

RIA systems should also have an in-built monitoring, evaluation and refinement mechanism in place. This includes early plans for data collection or access to data. Measuring and demonstrating the added value of RIA is also helpful in maintaining sustainable commitment for RIA. The measurement can also be used as a means to create healthy competition and a "market" for good RIA by acknowledging ministries that are performing well in their RIA implementation. The development of monitoring mechanisms to evaluate the success of the policy proposal and to feed that information into the development of future regulatory responses.

A regular, comprehensive evaluation of the impact of RIA on the (perceived) quality of regulatory decisions is essential. One area of useful data being collected by some central oversight bodies is the number of initial regulatory proposals that have been improved as a consequence of RIA and the estimated marginal increase in expected societal benefits. Governments should produce reports periodically providing numbers on RIAs produced over a certain period, summarising their quality (completeness of the analysis, coverage of all impacts, use of alternatives, comprehensiveness of stakeholder engagement) and also their impact on the quality of decisions being made, as well as the effectiveness and efficiency of the overall RIA framework.

In some cases, a parliamentary committee reviews RIA documents and can seek further information regarding the analysis. This function also constitutes a content-based form of *ex post* review of RIA. A further form of content based *ex post* review is provided by the courts, which can constitute an important check on the use of regulatory power in some countries (notably the United States). Again, a finding that the RIA is substantially inadequate has the potential in some countries to be deemed to be a material procedural inadequacy and lead to the regulation being invalidated. Thus, the prospect of court action can constitute an important quality assurance mechanism for RIA.

It is important to evaluate the impacts in cases where the original RIA document does not coincide with the final text of the proposal due to changes further down the legislative process (especially in parliaments).

In addition, **systematic evaluation of the performance of the regulatory oversight bodies** that co-ordinate and supervise the regulatory governance cycle, and oversee the quality of RIAs **is also important**. Such an evaluation process could contribute to the understanding of emerging problems and to the continuous learning of how to improve the practice of regulatory oversight.

Notes

[1] Administrations should only intervene when necessary.

[2] Regulations should lead to achieving its goals.

[3] Proposed solutions should be appropriate to the risk posed, and costs identified and minimised.

[4] The processes and rules for developing, amending and reviewing regulations should be clearly set and followed consistently.

[5] Administrations should be open, and keep regulations simple and user-friendly.

[6] Administrations must be able to justify decisions, and be subject to public scrutiny.

[7] Both regulations and regulation-making processes should be simple and easy to understand.

[8] All stakeholders should have an opportunity to express their views.

[9] So far, this approach has not been implemented in practice in any OECD country, according to our knowledge.

[10] Such as the Danish Business Forum.

[11] This should nonetheless be accompanied by an equally important requirement - ensuring that the data and evidence procured, collected and used in the RIA reflects the imperative of (i) impartiality and (ii) excellence.

[12] The following list is not prescriptive and present only potential options implementation of which depends on a legal and administrative system of a given country.

[13] And, potentially, having a member of the opposition to chair it, or members of non-government parties to sit in the body's board.

[14] Using this option depends on the legal an administrative system of the country.

[15] For a description of the Regulatory Governance Cycle, see (OECD, 2002[5]).

[16] However, it has also been argued that the use of external expertise (e.g. through the appointment of consultants) is not necessarily inconsistent with the achievement of the cultural change objectives in respect of RIA that were cited above. In this view, the fundamental issue is that of the nature of the relationship between the consultant and the policy officials: where the RIA consultant is brought into the policy process at an early stage, the relationship with departmental officials can be one of dialogue in which the work undertaken on the RIA can contribute to ongoing policy development, while also allowing for the transfer of expertise to departmental officials as part of the process. Arguably, there is little operational difference between the employment of an external policy consultant and the use of departmental staff, who can be considered to amount effectively to internal consultants. In both cases, the fundamental issue remains that of ensuring a direct and continuing dialogue between the RIA expert and departmental policy officials and decision-makers.

Still, administrations remain politically accountable and operationally and substantially responsible for the RIA. If they opt for outsourcing (parts of) a RIA, they should i) retain full control of the purpose, scope, and depth of the analysis; ii) be fully aware of the implications that the recommended option is likely to trigger; and iii) ascertain that the final proposed legal text reflects the RIA (and vice-versa). Ideally, any outsourcing should occur upon carefully drafted and validated protocols (Terms of Reference) to the attention of the contracting party – and such protocols should be made public. The selection of the contracting party (consultants, experts) must also be transparent and based on excellence.

[17] For example in Switzerland, a more complex RIA is required when three criteria from a list of 10 are met.

[18] E.g. the Australian Commonwealth Regulatory Burden Measure: https://rbm.obpr.gov.au/home.aspx.

[19] Where exceptions are invoked (and to reduce the incentive for their misuse), it should be mandatory to conduct an *ex post* evaluation in such cases. Data arrangements to monitor the regulation's impacts must be made at the time the regulation passes into law at the latest. This could be facilitated via a post-implementation review that is currently part of a number of countries' systems.

References

Adelle, C. et al. (2015), "New development: Regulatory impact assessment in developing countries—tales from the road to good governance", *Public Money & Management*, Vol. 35/3, pp. 233-238, http://dx.doi.org/10.1080/09540962.2015.1027500. [1]

Dudley, S. et al. (2017), "Consumer's Guide to Regulatory Impact Analysis: Ten Tips for Being an Informed Policymaker", *Journal of Benefit-Cost Analysis*, Vol. 8/02, pp. 187-204, http://dx.doi.org/10.1017/bca.2017.11. [4]

OECD (2019), *The Path to Becoming a Data-Driven Public Sector*, OECD Digital Government Studies, OECD Publishing, Paris, https://dx.doi.org/10.1787/059814a7-en. [3]

OECD (2019), *Tools and Ethics for Applied Behavioural Insights: The BASIC Toolkit*, OECD Publishing, Paris, https://dx.doi.org/10.1787/9ea76a8f-en. [6]

OECD (2018), *Cost-Benefit Analysis and the Environment: Further Developments and Policy Use*, OECD Publishing, Paris, https://dx.doi.org/10.1787/9789264085169-en. [7]

OECD (2015), "Regulatory Impact Assessment and regulatory policy", in *Regulatory Policy in Perspective: A Reader's Companion to the OECD Regulatory Policy Outlook 2015*, OECD Publishing, Paris, https://dx.doi.org/10.1787/9789264241800-5-en. [2]

OECD (2014), *OECD Regulatory Compliance Cost Assessment Guidance*, OECD Publishing, Paris, https://dx.doi.org/10.1787/9789264209657-en. [8]

OECD (2014), *Regulatory Enforcement and Inspections*, OECD Best Practice Principles for Regulatory Policy, OECD Publishing, Paris, https://dx.doi.org/10.1787/9789264208117-en. [9]

OECD (2002), *Regulatory Policies in OECD Countries: From Interventionism to Regulatory Governance*, OECD Reviews of Regulatory Reform, OECD Publishing, Paris, https://dx.doi.org/10.1787/9789264177437-en. [5]

www.ingramcontent.com/pod-product-compliance
Lightning Source LLC
LaVergne TN
LVHW062001070526
838199LV00060B/4227